Quotes for Personal Excellence – 2

Happiness

One Hundred Quotes and Thoughts
with One Hundred Insightful Illustrations of Lord Ganesha

R.N. Kogata • Lalita Kogata

PRINTWORLD
Publishers of Indian Traditions

First Published in India, 2014
ISBN 13: 978-81-246-0670-4
ISBN 10: 81-246-0670-6

A creation of:
Mr R.N. Kogata and Mrs Lalita Kogata
608, Hiran Magari, Sector - 11, Udaipur, India
Phones: +91-94141 58870, +91-294-258 3870
devkush@rediffmail.com

Printed and published by:
D.K. Printworld (P) Ltd.
'Vedasri', F-395, Sudarshan Park
(Metro Station: Ramesh Nagar), New Delhi - 110 015
Phones: 011-2545 3975 / 2546 6019 Fax: 011-2546 5926
e-mail: indology@dkprintworld.com Web: www.dkprintworld.com

Preface

Happiness is a feeling of peace; it is the gratification of the heart and soul. It constitutes a sense of peace and satisfaction, of gladness and enchantment, of fulfilment and tranquillity, of calm and serenity. It is an internal realization and can only be realized from within. No amount of outward success can bring us satisfaction and no amount of pleasure pursuits can make us happy if we are not at peace inside.

Happiness is often confused with pleasure. Pleasure is an enjoyable or agreeable sensation or emotion, amusement, recreation or gratification of the senses. It is derived from outside sources and is short lived. Happiness, on the other hand, is a feeling of joy or gladness, satisfaction and peace of mind, contentment and equanimity. It is an inner realization. One thing sure about happiness is that happiness is always possible and you always have ample reasons to be happy. Pleasure can never take the place of happiness.

All of us want to be happy and are looking for ways to be so. We want to unfold the secrets of happiness, which is our ultimate aim. No possession or achievement can have any meaning if it cannot make us happy. Happiness cannot be achieved by wrong means. We have to deserve it and deserve it right, with right action and purity of thoughts. No one else can make us happy. We have to learn to be happy ourselves. Challenging and skilled work with an element of competition can be very satisfying, stimulating, meaningful and a positive source of happiness. Positive actions will bring positive results as long as there are no negative motives behind them. We should also remember that happiness always rebounds on the giver.

To be truly happy, our work and achievements should be in consonance with our value systems and the meaning we have given to our lives, we have to be honest with our intentions and actions, from the bottom of our heart. It needs a solid base and an honest and harmonious character. It also needs us to be independent, courageous and co-operative. There is no end to wanting more and you should never postpone being happy in the hope of finding yourself in a better or perfect situation someday.

To be really happy and happy for a long time, just be careful about some basic rules. You should be willing to improve what you can and accept what you cannot improve or change. Worrying solves no problems and as long as you are worrying you cannot be happy. You should not allow public opinion to dominate your lives and criticism should not put you down. Forgiveness liberates you from the thoughts of anger and resentment, whereas holding back anger and resentment burn you from inside.

Your peace of mind depends on your thoughts. If you try to keep your miseries to yourselves and hide them from the public eye, it adds to your sense of unhappiness. Live your life with integrity and according to your conscience, your wants and your needs, and remember that the problems are a part of life. Remember, life is beautiful and you have only one life to live.

Happiness is a state of mind, and as such, everyone expects it to be easily attainable, but we also know that this is not really so, unless we understand how to remain happy in all conditions. In order to support and show easy ways and means of getting happiness for our beloved readers, we have conceived the idea of this book with quotes on happiness, which should certainly teach you much more in a few hours than a lifetime of bumbling around and instantly benefit you.

This book is a compilation of 100 carefully chosen quotations on Happiness, created, modified and mixed. Some of the thoughts presented are ours and others are from the people who have stood by and worked for values; some were famous and others were ordinary people. We have acknowledged separately the persons who have been quoted, wherever we could remember. Our sincere thanks to all these great personalities and eminent writers, who have given such invaluable thoughts to this world. Any amendment/addition is most welcome from the readers.

Ganesha gives peace, prosperity and wisdom and, therefore, each of the quotes in this book has a painting of Lord Ganesha to inspire you. These paintings have been created by our professional artists keeping in mind the themes of individual quotes.

We prostrate before our parents Smt Kanchan Devi and Shri Bhairav Lal Kogata, and Smt Kamla Devi Nuwal and the late Prof. K.M. Nuwal for their benign blessings for enabling us reach where we are.

With the expectation of blessings and constructive feedback from all our readers,

Lalita & R.N. Kogata

Acknowledgement

Quotations from some eminent writers, philosophers and great personalities have been included in this book. Details of the same are given below. We sincerely thank all of them.

Page No.	Quotation by	Page No.	Quotation by	Page No.	Quotation by
7	Bernard de Fontenelle	33	K. Moo	74	William Saroyan
8	Buddha	35	Agnes Repplier	76	Marcel Pagnol
10	Ella	36	Montesquieu	77	Graeme
11	Marcel Proust	39	Taisen Deshimaru	81	Freya Stark
12	Aristotle	44	Leo Tolstoy	82	Robert Brault
14	Levizzle	45	Albert Einstein	83	George Sand
15	Stacey Charter	46	Albert Schweitzer	84	Epictetus
16	Robert Brault	47	Sharon Salzberg	86	Eve
18	Wilson Kanadi	49	Isabella Giussani Mendieta	87	Helen Rowland
19	G.B. Shaw,	55	D. Julian	88	Mary Stuart
	Ralph Ingersoll,	57	Fyodor Dostoevsky	91	Mignon McLaughlin
	Rochefoucauld,	59	Douglas Horton	92	Philip F. Berstein
	James Oppenheir	60	Barbara de Angelis	93	Frederick Keonig
20	Eleanor Roosevelt,	63	Margaret Young	94	Colette
	Sydney J. Harris,	64	William Feather	95	Wilson Kanadi
	Immanuel Kant	65	Mort Walker	97	Helen Keller
21	Maxim Gorky	68	Roy Peng	99	Milton M. Toran
22	J.K. Rowling	69	Mark Amend	102	Mother Teresa
23	John Templeton	71	Albert Ellis	104	Vernon Howard
27	Mahatma Gandhi	72	Mark Twain	106	Lavetta Sue Wegman
30	Mark Amend	73	Eric Hoffer		

A great obstacle
to happiness
is to expect
too much happiness.

A single candle
can lighten a thousand candles
without waning its own light.

So happiness never decreases
as long as you share it.

Always . . . cherish all your happy moments.

They make a fine cushion for old age.

At times, I am glad that I am able to feel . . .
to be happy, sad, mad, confused,
frustrated, surprised and loved . . .

Because to feel these emotions is to learn,
to grow, to become a better person . . .
and I won't trade a single moment of pain felt . . .
for an ounce of joy . . .
because if I hadn't been able to feel that pain . . .

I won't be able to
fully appreciate the feeling
of true happiness.

Be grateful to people
who make you happy;

they are the charming gardeners
who make your soul blossom.

Being happy doesn't mean that everything around you is perfect.

It means that you have decided to look beyond the imperfections.

Better do what makes you happy.

If you spend whole of your life
trying to please others,
you are never going
to be happy.

Do not cry for what is lost.

Smile for what still remains.

Do not rely on someone else
for your happiness and self worth.
Only you can be responsible for that.

If you can't love and respect your own self,
no one else will be able to make that happen.

Accept who you are – completely;
the good and the bad and
make changes as you see befitting –
not because you think someone else
wants you to be different.

Enjoy the little things,
for one day you may look back
and realize that they were the big things.

Everyone has problems;

some people just show it off
more than the others.

Forget about your problems
and start to count
what you have right now.

You will realize
how great your God is!

Happiness

- is not a distant dream but is right under your own feet.
- held close is the seed; happiness shared is the flower.
- should not be consumed without producing it.
- is not in doing what you like, it is in liking what you do.
- can be achieved easily by making others happy.
- can be achieved easily by the wise, but not by the fools.
- has bad memory as its key.

Happiness

- is the road, not the destination.
- is not a dream; it is a way of life.
- is not the goal; it is a by-product.
- is not an ideal of reason, but of pure imagination.
- is not something you experience, it is something you remember.

Happiness always looks small
while you hold it close to your heart,

but let it go,
you will learn at once
how big and precious it was.

Happiness can be found,
even in the darkest of times,
if one remembers to
turn the light on.

Happiness comes from the spiritual wealth,
not the material wealth.

Happiness comes from giving, not by taking.

If you try to bring happiness to others,
one can't stop it from coming to you too.

To get joy, you must give it,
and to keep joy, you must scatter it.

Happiness is like a butterfly.
The more you chase it, the more it eludes you.

But if you turn your attention to other things
or sit down quietly,
it comes and sits softly down on your shoulder.

Happiness is like potato salad . . .
when shared with others, it's a picnic.

Happiness is not about having no problems.

It is about being able to enjoy something so greatly that you are able to forget about those problems, and move on smoothly in your life.

Happiness is when

- what you think,
- what you say, and
- what you do

are in complete harmony.

Happiness is when
you can smile . . .
with your heart.

Happiness is . . .
when you don't want to go to sleep
because reality is better than a dream.

Happy persons think
about all the people
in their lives . . .

Unhappy people think
about persons
not in their lives.

Happiness
that goes down to the heart
only lasts forever.

Happiness
will never come to those
who don't appreciate
what they already have.

I look back and see
all those lovely memories,
I wish I could go back
and relive them . . .

then I realize . . .

there are
more memories
to be made.

I smile when I see you,
I smile when I talk to you,
I smile when you touch me,
I smile when you are near me,
I smile when you look at me,
I smile when I think of you,
I smile for you.

But the one time I am truly happy
is when I make you smile back.

If it is not easy to find
happiness in yourself,

then it is not possible
to find it elsewhere.

If one only wished to be happy,
this could be easily accomplished;

but we always wish to be happier
than other people
and that is always difficult,
for we believe others look happier
than they really are.

If someone comes into your life
and becomes a part of you,
but for some reason he can't stay,
don't cry too much . . .

Just be glad that your paths were same for sometime
and somehow he made you happy
even for a while.

If tomorrow never comes,

I am so happy
I spent my today very well.

If you are not happy here and now,
you will never be.

If you are trapped between your feelings
and what other people think is right,
always go for whatever makes you happy . . .

unless, you want everybody
to be happy except you.

If you don't smile now,
you will hate yourself later.

If you get the chance
to make a wish,
and you realize
you have nothing to wish about –

that is when you know
you are really happy.

If you see someone
without a smile,

give him yours!

If you want to be happy
Let you BE . . . !

If you want to live
a happy life,

tie it to a goal,
not to people or things.

In the hope of reaching the moon,
men fail to see the flowers
that blossom at their feet.

It doesn't matter how long you may have been
stuck in a sense of your limitations.

If you go into a darkened room and put on the light,
it doesn't matter if the room has been dark
for a day, a week, or for years –
once you turn on the light, it is illuminated.

Once you expand your capacity
for love and happiness,
the light has been turned on forever!

It doesn't matter what others think about you.

What matters is what you think about yourself.

Don't be ashamed to do what brings you happiness.

Just be happy and ignore what others think about you.

It doesn't matter where you are,
as long as you are with the ones you love.

It doesn't matter how you spend your time,
as long as you spend it with the ones you love.

It doesn't matter as long as you enjoy the time
you spend with those you love.

As long as you are happy,
make happy all those you love.

It is better to create happiness than to pursue it.

It is the happiness
you find after some sadness
that makes life worthwhile.

It is up to you whether you walk through the day
with a smile on your face or with hate in your heart.

No one can give you happiness
but everyone can take it away, if you have it.

Because they themselves are jealous;
jealous because they can't smile like you.

So what's your choice, a giver or a taker?

Just keep smiling and pretending you are happy,
and then maybe after you have
convinced everyone else that you are happy,
you may convince yourself.

Slowly, it may become your habit
and finally your character.

Let a stranger give you a smile,
but never let a stranger take away your smile.

Let the only tears

that stream down your face

be those of joy!

Live life to the hilt;
take each moment as it comes.

Embrace the happy times and forget
the times that make you sad.

Life is too short to worry about
anything else but the good times.

So, wake up each day with a smile
and take the day as it comes!!!

Man is fond of counting his troubles,
but he doesn't count his joys.

If he counted them up as he ought to,
he would see that every lot of trouble
has enough happiness provided for it.

Maybe one day
you will realize
it isn't about being perfect,
it's about being happy.

No one can drive you crazy,
unless you yourself give him the key.

No one is in control of your happiness but you; therefore, you have the power to change anything about yourself or your life that you want to change.

Nobody is happy all the time,
but that is no excuse for being miserable.

Not many can make you smile,
too many can make you cry,

but it takes someone really special
to make you smile with tears in your eyes.

People often attempt to live their lives backwards;
they try to have more things,
or more money, in order to do more
of what they want, to see themselves happier.

The way it actually works is the reverse.

You must first be who you really are,
then do what you need to do,
in order to have what you want.

Plenty of people
miss their share of happiness,

not because they never found it,
but because they didn't make a stop
to enjoy it.

Seven days without laughter
makes one weak.

Smart people know their strengths,
but happy people are the ones
who have accepted their flaws.

Smile –
it's easier than explaining
why you are sad.

Smile today,
because tomorrow
you might not be able to.

Smiling is environment friendly.

It makes everyone's day
brighter and requires
very little energy.

Some cause happiness
wherever they go.

Others
whenever they go.

The best time of your life is when
you decide your problems are your own.

You don't blame your mother,
your kin or anyone else.

You realize that
you will have to control
your own destiny.

The best way
to cheer yourself up
is to try to cheer
somebody else up.

The constant search for happiness
is one of the chief sources
of prolonged unhappiness.

The greatest happiness
you can have is
knowing that you don't
necessarily need
to search for happiness.

And it is there
within you.

The happiest people don't have
the best of everything.

They just make
the best of everything.

The reason people
find it so hard
to be happy is that

they always see the past
better than it was,
the present worse than it is,
and the future
less resolved than it will be.

The relationships that really matter
are the ones that
make you happy and peaceful.

The secret of happiness is to make others believe that they are the cause of it.

The way to happiness:

Keep your heart free from hate, mind free from worry.
Live simple, expect little, give much.
Fill your life with love.
Scatter sunshine.
Forget yourself, think of others.
Do as you would be done by.
Try this for a week;
you will be surprised.

There are two ways of being happy –
Either diminish your wants
or augment your means.

There can be no happiness
if the things we believe in
are different from
the things we do.

There is no expert
on what happiness is,
but many on what
it might have been.

There is only one
great happiness
in this life,
to love and be loved.

There is only one way to happiness,
and that is to cease worrying about things
which are beyond our reach
and the power of our will.

Think this way:

We have one life, very limited time,
plenty of opportunities, plenty of blessings.

We should look at the best moments,
treasure as many pleasant memories as possible,
look for adventures, be random,
not listen to bad compliment,
treasure good one, and enjoy life,
because when you get old
what you want to remember
is the good times.

So, go and enjoy yourself
and try to make yourself happy!!!

To be happy there are two things we must forget . . .

The good things we do to others, and
the bad things that others do to us.

To be happy with a man,
you must understand him a lot
and love him a little.

To be happy with a woman,
you must love her a lot
and not try to understand her at all.

Try to:

be kind to all,
like many and love a few,
be on their stride,

because they are the nearest
to bring you happiness and help.

Today I am happy
because I realized how lucky I am
for everything that I have.

Today I am happy
because I don't have any reason
not to be.

Treasure every loving moment that you have and remember that time waits for no one.

Life is too short to be sad, depressed, stressed or just unhappy.

Look at all the things you have got – your dreams, your life, your love, your friends, the sunshine up above. Everything is okay now; so what are you worrying about?

Stop bothering yourself when there are so many reasons to be happy.

Do not worry about the mess today, just fix it tomorrow and relax.

Work like you don't need the money, love like you have never been hurt and dance as if no one is watching.

We are seldom happy
with what we now have,
but would go to pieces
if we lost any part of it.

Contentment is the answer.

We don't have any right to ask when sorrow comes,
"Why did this happen to me?"

Unless we ask the same question
for every joy that comes our way.

We tend to forget that
happiness doesn't come
as a result of getting something
we don't have, but
rather of recognizing and appreciating
what we do have.

What a wonderful life
I have had!

I only wish
I had realized it sooner.

What is the point of chasing happiness
if it costs the happiness
you have now?

When one door of happiness closes,
another one opens.

But often we look so long
at the closed door that
we don't see the one
that has been opened for us.

When I was in the grade school,
they told me to write down
what I wanted to be when I grew up.

I wrote down "happy".

They told me
"I didn't understand the assignment";
I told them
"they didn't understand life".

When you can admire
without desiring,
you will know
true happiness.

Why am I smiling?

Because I didn't see my name in the morning obituaries.

Worry doesn't help resolving
tomorrow's troubles,
but it does ruin
today's happiness.

You are only one thought away
from feeling good and happy.

You can't always
have happiness,

but you can always
give happiness.

You can't eat happiness. You can't buy it. You can't wear it. You can't drive it, or drink it, or sell it, or steal it. You can't lock it away. You can't negotiate for it. You can't win it, you can't marry it, you can't inherit it and you can't cheat it. You can't smoke it, or inject it, or rent it or borrow it. You can't campaign for it or beg for it, or talk other people into giving you theirs.

You can live happiness. You can create it. You can be it. You can give it to others. You can enjoy it. You can share it. You can claim it. You can have as much as you wish. You can enjoy it as much as you want, at any time, under any circumstance. You can work with it, play with it, worship, travel, eat and sleep with it.

Happiness is yours to live and yours to give, if only you will. It comes from within, and the best way to experience it is to let it flow out. Forget about trying and striving to get happy. Just decide to be happy, and happiness is yours.

You have succeeded in life
when all you really want
is only what you really need.

You know why it is hard to be happy?

It is because
we refuse to let go of the things
that made us sad.

You need to learn
to be happy by nature,
because
you will seldom have
the chance to be happy
by circumstances.